Finding Gold

by Connie Meyer

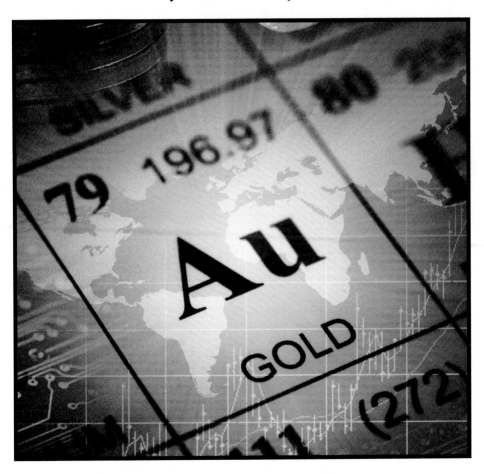

HOUGHTON MIFFLIN   BOSTON

King Tut's facemask was made of gold.

Gold. Shiny gold. People use gold to make things. Long ago, people made coins and art with gold. Look at the mask in the picture. It is a famous piece of gold. It is the facemask of King Tut. He was a boy who was king of Egypt.

People still like gold. We still make things from it. We like to look at gold. It is still worth a lot.

Gold is Special

I learned about gold in science class. Now I love gold! Here is what I know about gold. Gold is an element. Elements are made from little things called particles. Most things have many kinds of particles. Elements have only one kind of particle. Elements cannot change into anything else. If you heat gold, it is still gold. If you break it, it is still gold. Gold is also very heavy.

Gold is an element. Its symbol is Au.

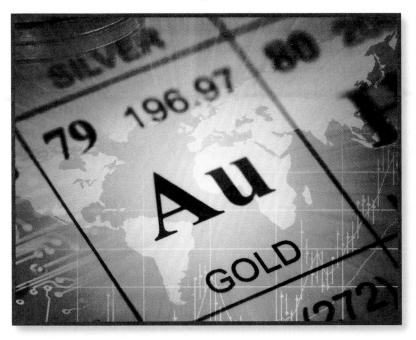

These miners hoped to find gold.

The Gold Rush

I cannot stop thinking about gold. I learned more about gold in social studies class. In 1848, a man found gold in California. His piece of gold was the size of a dime. People got excited. They wanted to find gold, too. They came from all over the world. They rushed to California. It was called the California Gold Rush. Only a few people found gold, though. I want to find gold!

People still find small amounts of gold today. There is some gold in California. There is some in other states. There are rules to look for gold. You must get permission.

It also helps to know science. I know science. I will tell you how to find gold.

You can still find gold today.

Looking for Gold

Hills and valleys are good places to look for gold. There are streams in hills and valleys. Look in streams where the water moves slowly. Do not look in fast streams. Fast water has a lot of force. It will push the gold away from you.

There could be gold in this California stream.

A miner looks for gold in the bottom of the pan.

Looking for gold in water is called panning for gold. Why? You need a big round pan.

A gold pan has a flat bottom. Gold is heavy. It is the heaviest element. It sinks to the bottom of the pan.

Light things float. The gold pan has slanted sides. The sides help separate light things from heavy things. The light things float out of the pan with the water.

The first thing you do is put your pan in the water.

Using the Pan

Here is how to pan for gold. Dip the pan into a stream. Fill it with many things. Fill it with sand, gravel, mud, and water. Now, shake the pan back and forth. This will help separate the light things from the heavy things. The heavy things will sink.

Tilting the pan lets sand and gravel fall out.

Now you can filter out the gold. To filter is to separate. Tilt the pan in the stream. Keep it under the water. Pull it up and shake it. The light sand and gravel rise to the top. They go out of the pan with the water.

These people pan for gold in a stream.

Make a Wave

Next, hold the pan flat. Tip it slowly. The water swirls around in the bottom corner. You have made a wave. The wave stirs things in the pan. It pushes the light things to the top. It moves the heavy things around on the bottom.

Try to put the right amount of water in the pan. Too much water moves everything. You do not want the heavy things to move. They should stay in the pan. Too little water does not move anything. Put your finger in the water. You should feel things swirling in the pan.

There are gold nuggets in this pan!

Gold showed up after swirling the water in this pan.

Seeing the Gold

Dip the edge of the pan down. Make a big angle. Tilt it more. Then swirl it around again. Now, look at the bottom of the pan. There will be a small pile left. Look in the pile. Is there gold in the pile? Gold is yellow. It will be easy to see.

How does panning for gold work? Gold is heavy. It sinks to the bottom of the pan. The sand and rocks from the stream are lighter. The swirling water makes them float. The heavy gold stays on the bottom of the pan. Then you can find it there.

Gold nuggets sink to the bottom of the pan.

This is an example of gold leaf.

What is Gold?

Gold is pretty. It is also special in other ways. It does not change color. It always looks new. Gold is very strong. It can be made into thin wire. Gold wire can be many miles long. It does not break. Gold can also be pounded very thin. This thin gold is called gold leaf. It is as thin as a leaf.

This fool's gold is shiny, but it isn't real gold.

When you look for gold, be careful. You can be fooled by fool's gold. Fool's gold looks like real gold. It is different, though. How can you tell the difference? Rub the piece of gold on the back of a white tile. Fool's gold leaves a green or black mark. Real gold leaves a yellow mark.

Saving your money may be the easiest way to get gold!

Science class helped me learn about gold. Too bad it did not help me find gold! I had fun panning for gold. I only found a few tiny bits, though. They were the size of a grain of sand. Now I know a better way to find gold. I will save my money. Then I will buy some gold!